**W9-BGF-839**

More praise for Rachelle Doorley's *Creative Adventures in Cursive:*

"In this age of over-developed thumbs flying over tiny keyboards, this guide to joyful handwriting takes the curse out of cursive and reconnects young writers' hands with their eyes and minds. Doorley unabashedly embraces the aesthetic dimension of learning—the powerful attraction we have to making what we produce, especially our words and ideas, beautiful on the page. The nearly lost art of handwriting is recovered here with countless activities and exercises designed to excite and engage young learners."

—Steve Seidel, Director of the Arts in Education Program at the
Harvard Graduate School of Education

CREATIVE ADVENTURES IN

CREATIVE ADVENTURES IN

Cursive

WRITE WITH GLUE, STRING, MARKERS, PAINT, AND ICING

RACHELLE DOORLEY

QUARRY

© 2018 Quarto Publishing Group USA Inc.
Text and Artwork © 2018 Rachelle Doorley

First Published in 2018 by Quarry Books, an imprint of The Quarto Group, 100 Cummings Center, Suite 265-D, Beverly, MA 01915, USA.
T (978) 282-9590 F (978) 283-2742 QuartoKnows.com

Quarry Books titles are also available at discount for retail, wholesale, promotional, and bulk purchase. For details, contact the Special Sales Manager by email at special-sales@quarto.com or by mail at The Quarto Group, Attn: Special Sales Manager, 401 Second Avenue North, Suite 310, Minneapolis, MN 55401, USA.

10 9 8 7 6 5 4 3 2 1

ISBN: 978-1-63159-477-9

Digital edition published in 2018

Library of Congress Cataloging-in-Publication Data available

Design: Debbie Berne
Cover Image: Glenn Scott Photography
Photography: Rachelle Doorley
Illustration: Rachelle Doorley

Printed in China

This book is dedicated to my mom, Sheila Anthony,
a magnificent role model with a knack for graceful script.

Contents

introduction

hen I was in school, cursive was taught to all children at around age eight or nine. Learning this flowing, sophisticated style of writing was challenging and fun. When I discovered that I could dress up these beautiful letters with loops and swirls, it became creative, too. Cursive writing opened up new adventures in self-expression for me, and I can vividly remember the joy of practicing my lettering and experimenting with writing my name and then names of my friends with sweeping embellishments.

Although it was new to me back then, cursive, which is also known as script, longhand, and handwriting, has been around for hundreds of years. Kings and queens, explorers and spies, and presidents and founding fathers wrote their important documents and secret messages in cursive. Some of these are shared throughout the book as starting points of inspiration.

Cursive was originally invented with the intention of making writing quicker. Because cursive forms when letters connect together, you don't have to pick up your pen or pencil as often as you do when you print, and that can save time.

But cursive is also a wonderful means of self-expression. Each of our handwriting styles is different, and everyone's signature is unique. Those things let us share our personalities with the world in ways that writing on a keyboard can't. When we hand write our name on something, we make it personal. When we send a handwritten note to a friend, it contains a little bit of ourselves that can be special to the person who receives it.

And there's more! Writing by hand can help you think! Some people think, "Why write in cursive when you can write on a laptop?" But taking notes down by hand allows you to learn them better and remember them better than writing on a computer!

In this book, you'll try out your cursive skills in ways you never imagined. You'll find out how to write with icing, yarn, clay, needle and thread, and paint. You'll find out how to write on rocks, write on balloons, make things for your room, make good things to eat, and even invent your own writing style!

Cursive is fun, and the adventure begins here.

1

All About Writing

Cursive Warm-ups

tips

Make sure your work area is clear of clutter.

Relax your hand: Don't grip too hard because this can add stress to your hand. When your hand is relaxed, you have more freedom to make flourishes and loose writing.

Move your arm and wrist to the right as you write. A static hand will make your writing wobbly.

Is cursive writing a sport? Well, maybe not, *but* in just the same way that we warm up our bodies before playing sports, it can be helpful to warm up your arms and hands before tackling a session of writing. A little warm-up will let you feel relaxed and ready for tackling a project with script, scrolls, and scrawls. Try these stretches and doodling exercises that are not only good warm-ups, but just plain fun.

Warm-up Exercises

Hand and arm warm-ups

- Tighten your hands into fists and then open your hands, stretching your fingers wide.

- Touch each of your fingers to your thumb.

- Roll your wrists—outward five times, then inward five times.

- Hold one arm out and squeeze your wrist with the other hand. Then, move up the arm, gently squeezing as you go. Switch arms and repeat.

- Rub your hands together.

- Intertwine your fingers and squeeze your hands together a few times.

Writing exercises

- Set out a piece of paper and pick up your pencil or pen.

- Start making an *o* and then keep making it across the paper. Now, make *o's* in the other direction. Make *o's* that get smaller as they move across the page.

- Make rows of zigzags across the paper.

- Without picking up your pen, make a running line of *f's* across the page. Allow for plenty of space between letters. Try this with other letters, too!

- Draw a circle with a pencil and make cursive *f's* all the way around the circle so it forms a lacy wreath. Do the same with *l's* and *e's*.

- Draw a spiral in pencil and then write over it with a message in cursive.

CREATE YOUR OWN

Cursive Style

You'll Need

☐ blank paper

☐ pencils or pens

Why not experiment with different cursive styles that suggest who you are. Will your style be careful, bold, old fashioned, or charming? With a little bit of practice, you can design a style that's all you. The best way to find your own style is to keep on practicing. After experimenting with these two exercises, develop your style by writing a letter to a friend.

#1 Write a Pangram Sentence

A pangram is a sentence that includes all the letters of the alphabet. It's a great tool for practicing your cursive and seeing how all the letters will look.

Try one of these pangrams on a new page:

1   The quick brown fox jumps over the lazy dog.

2   The five boxing wizards jump quickly.

Here are examples of cursive pangrams.

The quick brown fox jumps over the lazy dog.

The quick brown fox jumps over the lazy dog.

The quick brown fox jumps over the lazy dog.

The quick brown fox jumps over the lazy dog

The quick brown fox jumps over the lazy dog

#2 Design Your Own Signature

Give yourself some time and write lots and lots of trials of your name.

1 Fill your page with different versions of your name.

2 Experiment, try new things, and add flourishes.

3 Keep experimenting until you find something you like.

4 Once you've got it, fill another page with your new signature.

Write your name in cursive, slanting right.

Write your name in cursive with no slant.

Write your name in cursive, slanting left.

Write your name like you are a really joyful person.

Write your name like you are a really silly person.

Write your name like you are a really excited person.

Write your name like you are a really sleepy person.

Write loopy cursive.

Write cramped cursive.

Write with fancy stars or flowers.

Flourishes, Swashes, and Vines

You'll Need

- ☐ paper
- ☐ pencil, pens, and markers

Decorative curls and fanciful flourishments make your cursive extra fancy and special. You can think of them as jewelry for your words. The curly strokes that are attached to letters are called *swashes*. They've been used in writing since at least the 1500s!

Drawing flourishes and swashes takes a little practice. The important thing is to keep your hand relaxed while working quickly. Once you get the swing of it, you can invent new swashes and combine them in your very own creative ways.

Steps

1 Make a practice sheet of flourishes, swashes, and vines.

2 Look at the examples on these pages for inspiration. Copy these and invent your own.

3 Add your flourishes to any of the projects in this book.

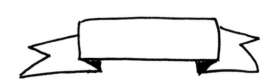

Flourishes

Vines

17

Make a Feather Quill

The shaft, or hollow part, of a feather is called a *quill*. Long before laptops or even pencils, markers, and ballpoint pens, people used quills—large feathers with a sharpened end—to write with. (Rita Skeeter had one in the Harry Potter movies.) Quills work surprisingly well. If you have the opportunity to look at important documents written before the 19th century, you'll see what quills can do.

To this day, the United States Supreme Court maintains a tradition day of placing white quills on counsel tables each time the Court is in session. Lawyers who appear in court can take these quills home as souvenirs. The good news is that quills aren't too difficult to make, and you can have your very own quill without showing up in court!

"Using a feather quill is a slower method of writing than using a pen and you need to refresh your quill a lot!" —Nola

You'll Need

- [ ] jar of water (for soaking feathers)
- [ ] large feathers such as those from geese, turkeys, and ducks. (Any feather that is long enough to hold like a pen will do the trick.)
- [ ] fine white sand (from the craft store)
- [ ] aluminum can
- [ ] baking sheet
- [ ] oven
- [ ] optional: knife
- [ ] optional: sandpaper
- [ ] very sharp scissors
- [ ] tweezers
- [ ] washable black ink
- [ ] paper

Temper the Quill

1   First, you need to temper (harden) the quill. This will remove any excess oil and will help you make a clean cut when you create the writing point.

2   Soak the end of the quill in water overnight.

3   Fill the can with sand, place it on a baking sheet, and heat it in an oven set to 350°F (180°C or gas mark 4). Bake for 20 minutes.

4   Carefully remove the can from the oven (it will be hot!) and gently press the wet quill into the sand as far as it will go.

5   Remove the quill once the sand cools.

Strip the Feathers

1   If there are vanes or downy feather barbs close to the tip, where you'll hold the quill, you can peel them away or have an adult help you strip away some of the vanes with a knife.

2   Test to see if you can get a comfortable grip on the quill, just as you would grip a pencil.

"I liked using a split quill once I got used to it." —Naomi

"I prefer not splitting the quill because it splatters and makes it harder to write." —Hannah

"Not splitting the quill is easier for me because when I write sideways it messes the writing up." —Cecilia

Make the Nib
(the Point for Writing)

You might want to ask an adult to help you with this part. The cuts have to be made just right.

1 Make sure you can hold the quill without the vanes getting in the way. Experiment with the quill to find the most natural way to hold it.

2 Mark the tip for where the writing point should be.

3 Sand the area that you'll hold, if you like. Sanding will help give you a good grip.

4 Cut the tip of the quill at a slant of 45 degrees or less to shape the nib.

5 Use tweezers to remove the loose material from inside the hollow quill.

6 Cut the very end of the nib flat.

7 Carefully cut a slit down the middle of the nib (optional).

8 Dip the pen in ink and practice writing. Practice drawing. Practice making drips and splats. You'll feel like someone from another century.

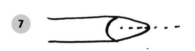

"If you write with the tip, you can make a thinner line and switch to a thicker line by changing the angle of the quill. Also, you can flick the quill to make splatters, but be sure your table is covered if you try this!" —Hannah

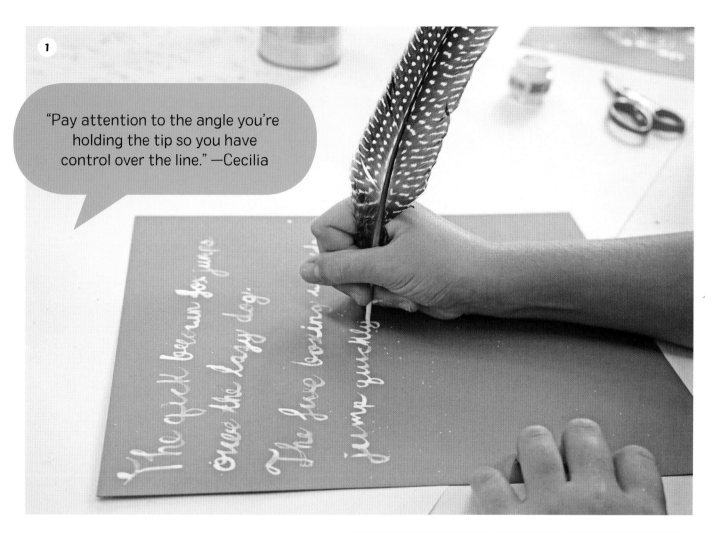

1

"Pay attention to the angle you're holding the tip so you have control over the line." —Cecilia

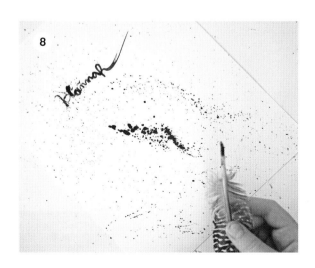

8

8

Bullet Journal

You'll Need

- ☐ dot or grid journal
- ☐ black felt tip pen
- ☐ markers in different colors
- ☐ optional tools: dividers, divider tabs, stencils, washi tape, ruler, and rubber stamps and ink pads

Do you like to doodle in sketchbooks? Keep a diary? Make lists of things you want (or have) to do? Then you just might be a bullet journaler. A bullet journal is a notebook where you use bullet points (dots and symbols) to organize your ideas, keep track of what you've done and what still needs doing, and make all your notes easy to find. But it's better than that: As you work in it, your bullet journal becomes a wonderful record of your own creativity—a place where you can test out new ideas in private and discover the artist, writer, inventor, and dreamer inside of you!

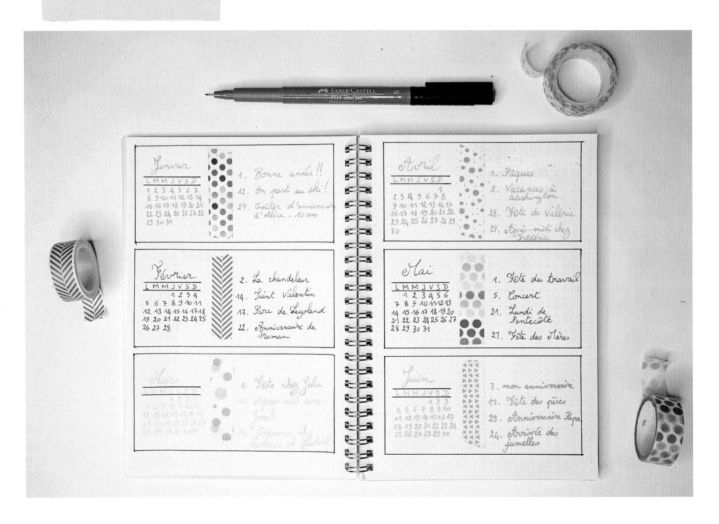

Getting Started

The first thing to do is number all the pages, starting with "1" on the first page.

First Page

Decorate the first page with your name and phone number (in case your journal gets lost). You might also attach one of your bookplates (see page 28).

Index

On page two, start an index. Think of the index as a table of contents that will help you find pages and notes that you are looking for. Your index will continue to grow as your journal grows—so you'll need at least two pages for it. Write "Index" at the top of those pages.

Year at a Glance

If you want to keep track of your year, on the next four pages (two spreads), create a calendar of upcoming months and fill in any events that you know about such as birthdays, school holidays, or vacations. To make your calendar, divide each of the four pages into three horizontal sections and label each section with the name of the next twelve months.

Everything in Order

You'll add pages to your journal as you think of them. These could be lists of to-do items, books that you want to read, birthday planning ideas, or simply pages of your drawings. When you start a new page, add it to your index and write down the corresponding page number. And don't forget—use your color markers to decorate the pages any way you like.

To-Do Lists

For to-do lists, the inventor of the bullet journal, Ryder Carroll, came up with symbols (the bullet points) that let you track your progress. Try this system out and see if it works for you, too!

.	task
<	task scheduled
>	task migrated (moved to another list)
–	note
X	complete
★	event

September 6

- . Write thank you notes
- < Bring cupcakes to school on Wednesday
- > Clean bedroom
- – We looked at puppies this weekend—so cute!
- X Study for math quiz
- ★ Erin's birthday party on Saturday

The list of things you end up including on your table of contents will be as personal as you are—no two bullet journals are alike, and that's a good thing.

Inspiration

Include banners.

Embellish corners with designs.

Make fancy dividers to break up the page.

Draw doodles to represent familiar ideas, such as a cake, a pencil, a tree, a house, some clouds, or a mountain.

Invent elaborate titles.

Put frames around ideas to help them pop out.

Add color to the page.

Make the date stand out with banners, bunting, or flourishes.

Add washi tape, stickers, and paint.

Illustrate the weather.

Page Ideas

Decorate the pages and have fun with your handwriting. You might use plain cursive for the to-do lists and fancy, scrolling script for your dreams and wish lists. Here are some ideas for some of the things you might want to include:

- Seasonal Bucket List
- Movie List
- Wish List
- Story Ideas
- Goals for the Year
- Birthdays
- Things That Make Me Happy
- I Want to Learn to . . .
- Page for the Month
- Weekly Calendar
- Favorite Songs
- Tough Spelling Words
- Words of the Day
- Daily Acts of Kindness
- Favorite Quotes
- Font Practice Sheet
- Monthly Memories
- Words of Wisdom
- Life Dreams
- Page of Icons
- Jokes and Riddles
- Poems
- Haiku
- Make a page of Page Ideas!

2

Gifts from the Heart

Bookplates

What's a bookplate? It's a decorative label with your name or someone else's that's glued inside a book. It's not only beautiful, but it announces who the book belongs to and reminds others where to return a book they've borrowed.

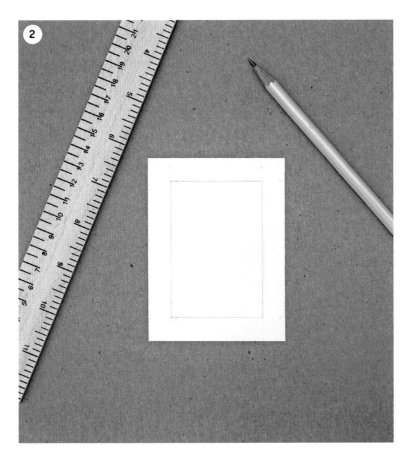

You'll Need

☐ card stock
☐ scissors or paper cutter
☐ ruler
☐ pencil
☐ marker, brush pen, or calligraphy pen

Steps

1   Cut the card stock to size. The bookplates shown here are 3.5 × 4 inches (9 × 10 cm).

2   Use your ruler and pencil to draw a ½ inch (1.3 cm) border along each side. Draw lightly so you can erase the guidelines later.

3   Decorate your border as you desire (see the three options that follow for some ideas).

4   Write a bookplate message in the middle of the frame.

(If the bookplates are for you, write your name on the dotted lines. If they're a gift, write the lucky giftee's name instead!)

5   Use a glue stick to attach the bookplates inside your favorite books.

Bookplate Message Ideas

The messages on bookplates often say, "This book belongs to:" or "From the library of:". But your message can say anything you like. Here are some ideas:

FROM THE AWESOME BOOKSHELF OF

FROM THE SECRET COLLECTION OF

THIS BOOK IS A GIFT FROM

A FAVORITE BOOK OF

FROM THE SCI-FI COLLECTION OF

#1 Dots

1 Squeeze a small amount of acrylic paint onto the paper plate.

2 Use cotton swabs to create a dotted frame.

You'll Need

☐ acrylic paint

☐ cotton swabs

☐ paper plate

tip

It's fun to write your message and your name extra fancy on a bookplate. Practice writing your name with scrolls and maybe a few swashes (see page 15). Then try out your skills on the bookplate.

#2 Collage

1. Cut the paper into ½" (1.3 cm) strips

2. Glue the strips onto the bookplate borders.

3. Trim away excess paper.

You'll Need

- ☐ colorful paper such as old maps, old art work, wrapping paper, or scrapbook paper
- ☐ glue stick
- ☐ scissors

#3 Watercolor

1. Fill in the bookplate borders with watercolor paint.

2. Paint a small section with one color. While the paint is still wet, paint another small area with a second color so that the colors overlap and bleed together. Continue on like this until the entire border is painted.

You'll Need

- ☐ watercolor paint
- ☐ 1 or more watercolor paintbrushes
- ☐ towel
- ☐ cup of water

Sculpey Plaques

Did you ever think you'd see your name as sculpture? Polymer clay is perfect for writing cursive in 3-D because it comes in so many colors and can be fired in your kitchen oven. These clay plaques are made by forming the clay into the shape of a name, a special word, or a favorite phrase and arranging that word onto a molded clay base.

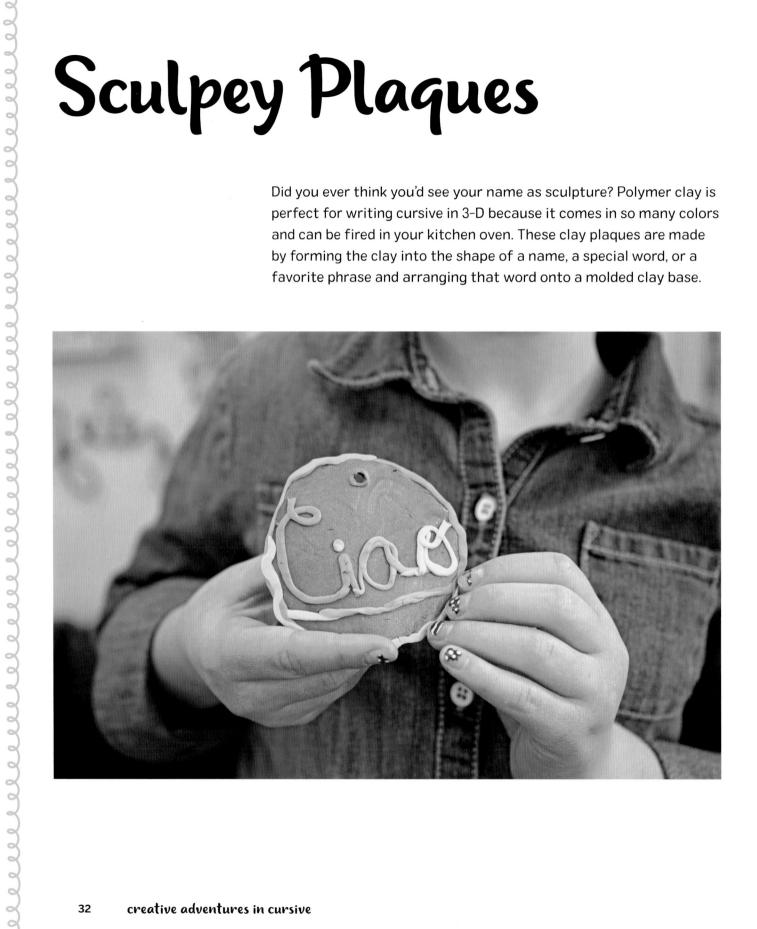

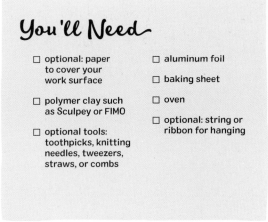

You'll Need

- ☐ optional: paper to cover your work surface
- ☐ polymer clay such as Sculpey or FIMO
- ☐ optional tools: toothpicks, knitting needles, tweezers, straws, or combs
- ☐ aluminum foil
- ☐ baking sheet
- ☐ oven
- ☐ optional: string or ribbon for hanging

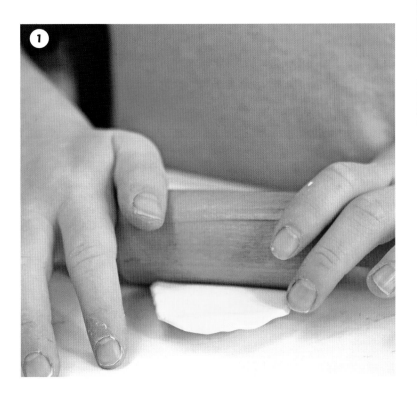

Steps

1 Polymer clay is very firm when you take it out of its package. The first thing you'll want to do is "condition" your clay, which is to soften it so that it's pliable. Roll it in different directions with a rolling pin or squish it with your fingers. The warmth of your hands should make the clay easy to use in a few minutes.

2 Roll out and flatten a piece of clay to make your base. Shape it into a circle, heart, or whatever you desire.

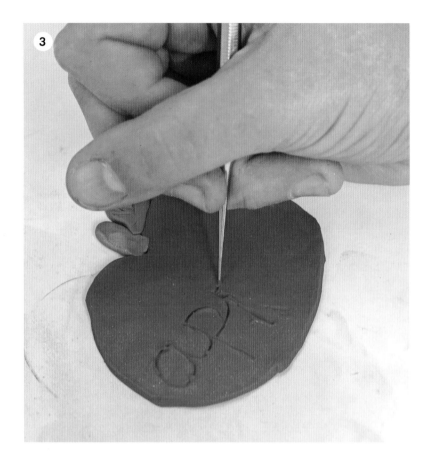

3   To make sure your word will fit on the base, sketch the word on the clay lightly with a pencil or stylus.

4   Roll a piece of clay into a long snake that's about ¼ inch (6 mm) in diameter. Twist and fold two or more strands of clay together to get mixed colors, or make several snakes in different colors.

5   Using cursive, form the clay into a word or name and place it on top of your base. Secure it by pressing the word edges into the base.

6   If you wish, poke a hole in the base so that you can hang the plaque later.

7   Follow the manufacturer's directions for baking your clay.

8   Use an oven mitt to remove the baking sheet from the oven. Allow the baking sheet and clay to cool completely before you touch it.

9   Thread a ribbon through the hole and find the perfect spot to hang or display your name as cursive sculpture.

safety tips

Keep the tools you use for working with clay separate from the tools used for preparing food. If you use kitchen utensils as clay tools, be sure to label them "for clay only."

Be sure to wash your hands after using clay. If it's hard to remove from your hands, rub them with a little bit of cooking oil and then follow up with soap and water.

Clay can stain! Keep the clay away from clothes, upholstery, or rugs as it's hard to remove if it gets pressed into the fibers.

Work on top of waxed paper, paper, or foil if you're worried about the clay staining your tabletop or work surface.

Seed Packets

You'll Need

- ☐ packet of seeds
- ☐ small bowl or saucer
- ☐ scratch paper
- ☐ pencil
- ☐ scissors
- ☐ paper to make seed packet envelopes
- ☐ glue stick
- ☐ felt pens
- ☐ watercolor paint
- ☐ watercolor paintbrush
- ☐ cup of water

These packets are a thoughtful gift for springtime birthdays, Mother's Day, and even Easter. You can collect seeds from the plants in your garden or buy them from a garden center and then repackage them in your own hand-designed envelopes.

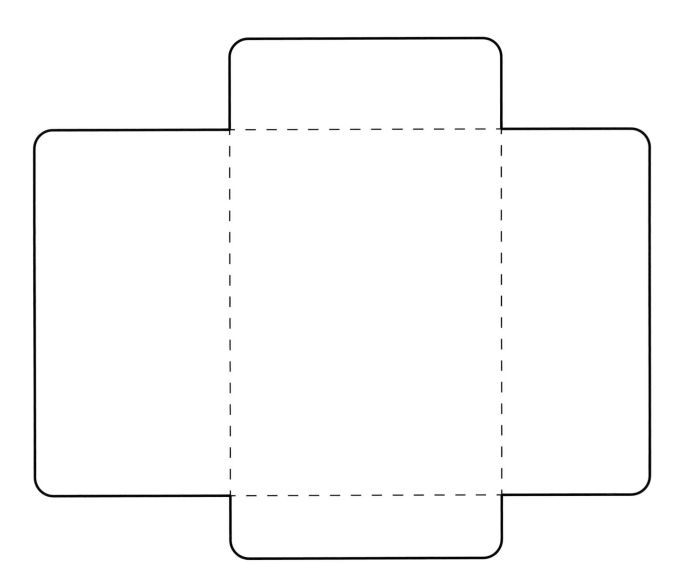

Steps

1 Make a template for your seed packets. If you are repackaging seeds that you've bought, open the packet carefully and empty the seeds into a bowl or saucer. Carefully undo the paper packet along the glued edges and open it out flat. Trace the shape of the packet onto a piece of scratch paper and mark the folds with dotted lines.

2 If you are using seeds from your garden, follow the same steps with any small envelope. You can also trace the template above.

3 Cut out the template.

"You should always use scratch paper so you don't accidentally mess up your work. And if you have tiny seeds, you could tape the bottom so they don't fall out." —Audrey

"When coloring these in, you can use whatever coloring tool you like!" —Amelia

4 Trace the template onto the paper for the seed packet envelope.

5 Cut out the envelope and fold it along the dotted lines.

6 Glue the packet along the back seam and bottom edge.

7 Practice writing your seed name on scratch paper in your best script. Perhaps match the color of your writing to the color of the flower or vegetable.

8 Write the seed name on the envelope.

9 Use watercolor paint to decorate the envelope with pictures of the flower or vegetable.

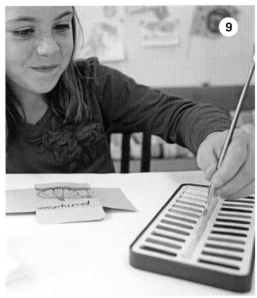

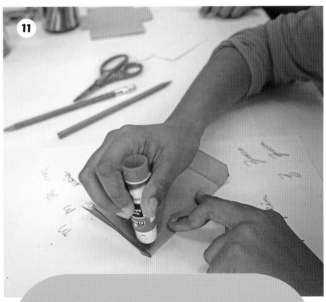

10 Wait until the paint is dry before putting the seeds inside.

11 Glue the envelope shut to seal the seeds inside.

"You could research different languages and write the seed names in other languages." —Amalia

Embroidered Napkin

How can cursive help you set the table? Here's how. Start with a beautiful cursive initial, embroidered on a fabric napkin, and then use it to dress up the family dinner table. You could create a whole set that includes one for each of your family members—for every day use or for special occasions.

Embroidery is done with a needle and a special thread called "floss" that comes in an amazing variety of beautiful colors. An embroidery hoop will help us keep the fabric smooth and tight while we make our stitches. Be creative and design your napkin with a single initial or with a fancy two- or three-initial monogram!

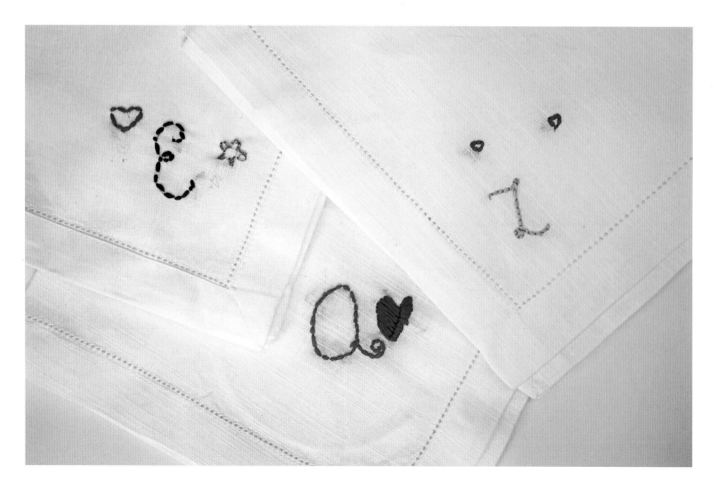

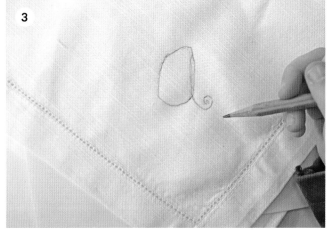

You'll Need

- [ ] pencil and paper
- [ ] cloth napkin
- [ ] optional: graphite paper for tracing
- [ ] embroidery hoop, 5" to 7" (12.5 to 18 cm)
- [ ] cotton embroidery floss
- [ ] embroidery needle
- [ ] optional: needle threader
- [ ] scissors

Steps

1 Draw a few practice letters until you get one that you like. Make your letter at least 2 inches (5 cm) tall so that it's easy to embroider.

2 Open the napkin and lay it flat on your work surface. Decide how big you'd like your cursive initial to be and where you want to place it on the napkin.

3 Draw the letter onto the napkin. Optional: You could use graphite paper to trace the letter onto the napkin.

6

Note on Curves

Curves are easy. Simply follow the curved line with the backstitch.

4 Separate the embroidery hoop into two pieces.

5 Place the napkin over the smaller, inner hoop.

6 Place the larger hoop on top and tighten the hoop until the fabric is taut. If there's any slack, open the hoop and adjust the fabric accordingly.

7 Thread the needle with 2 or 3 strands of floss and tie one end with a double knot. Use an embroidery needle threader to help, if needed.

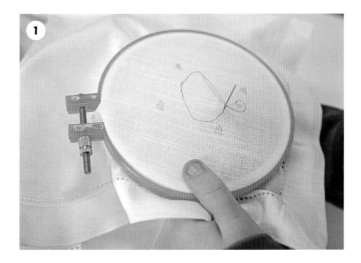

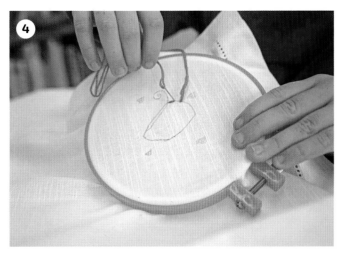

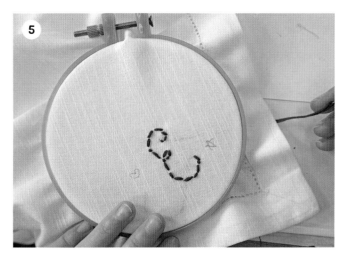

Backstitch Steps

There are a lot of beautiful embroidery stitches, and I would encourage you to try out other ideas once you get the hang of this one. We'll use the backstitch, which is an easy way to get a beautiful running line that can loop and turn.

1   Try to make nice small stitches, no more than ¼ inch (6 mm). Holding your threaded needle on the underside of the hoop, directly under your letter, poke the needle up through the fabric about ¼ inch (6 mm) in from one end of your letter. Pull the needle and thread through so the embroidery thread is taut.

2   Now, make your stitch going backward, inserting the needle at the very start of your letter, and pull the thread taut.

3   Following your pencil line, bring the needle up through the fabric again about ¼ inch (6 mm) beyond the first hole you made.

4   Again, make your stitch going backward, inserting the needle through that first hole.

5   Continue in this way. Each stitch coming up through the underside moves you ¼ inch (6 mm) further along your letter's outline. Each stitch, going from the top of the fabric to the underside, goes back through the previous hole.

6   When you complete the outline of your letter, knot the thread on the underside of the fabric.

3

Décor

Painted Rocks

Artist alert! Once you paint a few rocks, it can be hard to stop!

Paint names on rocks and use them as place settings at the dinner table. Write an inspiring word or message on a rock and give it to a friend or plant it in your garden.

Writing on rocks will give you the chance to practice fine writing, and small round paintbrushes will help you write with care—look for round paintbrushes that are size 0 or 1.

Note: If you don't happen to live by the shore or a stream, "river rocks," found in hardware or home improvement stores, are excellent for this project.

- ☐ newsprint or a plastic cover to protect your work surface
- ☐ smooth rocks
- ☐ flat, synthetic paintbrush
- ☐ white gesso
- ☐ acrylic paint in assorted colors
- ☐ small, round, synthetic paintbrush (size 0 or 1)
- ☐ cup of water
- ☐ practice paper
- ☐ Mod Podge or clear acrylic sealer

Steps

1 Cover your work area and set out the rocks.

2 Prime the rock: Using the flat paintbrush, paint a coat of gesso on the smoothest side of each rock. I recommend painting just one side of the rock to simplify this process, but you can paint the entire rock if you like. When the first coat of gesso dries completely, brush on one more coat. The brightness of the gesso will help the next coat of color paint show up vividly.

3 Paint the base color: Use the flat paintbrush to paint a color or colors on top of the gessoed areas on the rocks. If you can still see streaks once the paint is dry, you could add another coat.

4   To create a blended effect, use flat paintbrushes to paint two colors next to each other. While they are still wet, use one of the paintbrushes to blend the colors together where they meet. Allow the paint to dry completely.

5   Write your words. Choose a paint color that contrasts with the background. Use the small round paintbrush to write on your rock. If your rock is small, choose just one word or a short phrase. Add a picture if you like! Allow the paint to dry.

6   Use the flat paintbrush to coat your rocks with Mod Podge. This is will seal the paint and keep it from chipping off.

tips

· Writing with a paintbrush is a little messier than writing with a pen. Try practicing on scratch paper first!

· You might find it helpful to write the word in pencil on the rock first. Then, follow the pencil lines with your brushstrokes.

· If your writing isn't flowing easily with the paint-brush, the paint might be a little too dry. Mix a drop of water into your paint and then try writing again. Still too dry? Add another drop.

Doorplate

A doorplate is a nameplate that you hang on your door. But a nameplate doesn't have to feature your actual *name*—it can be whatever word captures who you are—your favorite sport, activity, or what you like to think about.

"Don't make your drawing too small because then it will be more difficult to paint." —Elise

You'll Need

- [ ] pencil (for drawing outline)
- [ ] scratch paper
- [ ] wood plaque from the craft store
- [ ] optional: graphite paper
- [ ] acrylic paint
- [ ] small, round, synthetic paintbrushes (size 0 or 1)
- [ ] flat, synthetic paintbrushes (a variety)
- [ ] optional: sandpaper
- [ ] screw eyes (from the hardware store) or low-heat glue gun
- [ ] ribbon or twine for hanging

Painting the Doorplate

1 Use the pencil and scratch paper to practice writing your name in cursive, the way you want it to appear on your door.

2 When you've got it just right, lightly write your word in your best script on the wood plaque with pencil.

3 Choose your paint colors and squeeze out a little of each on the plate. Mix the paint with a little bit of water so that it flows smoothly. Trace over your lines with the paint.

Variation

You can use graphite paper to transfer your name. Place the graphite paper on top of the plaque, graphite-side down. Place the sketch of your name on top of the graphite. Draw over your name with pencil to transfer it.

"If you want to get a sharp line for your word or picture, use a small, round brush. I used a size 1 brush. If you're filling in a larger space, use a small, flat brush like a ¼-inch (6 mm) brush (my favorite)." —Nola

4 If you like, choose a different color for each letter. If you can still see the pencil lines when the paint dries, go over the lines again. If you want your name to appear bolder, go back over your name again, this time thickening the lines.

5 Think about what kind of decoration to add to your plaque. When your name is dry, add decorative flourishes to make it truly special.

6 Stand back and admire your work!

tip

If any paint smudges in unwanted spots, wait until it dries and then use sandpaper to sand it back. Alternatively, just paint over the smudge with a design.

Adding Hardware

1 When the paint on your doorplate is dry, turn it face down on your work surface.

2 Attach the ribbon in one of the following ways:

a) If your doorplate is not too heavy, you can attach ribbon simply with a low-heat glue gun. Cut the ribbon to size, apply glue where you want it, and attach the ribbon while the glue is still hot.

b) If your doorplate is heavier, screw in two small screw eyes along the top of the plaque. Thread the ribbon through the screw eyes and secure it with a knot or bow.

Flourish Inspirations

Flowers	Leaves
Arrows	Hearts
Wreaths	Stars

Stenciled Pillow

Did you know it's possible to create your own stencils? This is such a fun process because you can use it to make pillows that look like they came right out of a furniture showroom. These special pillows are fun to make for your bedroom, family room, or as a gift for a loved one.

You'll Need

- ☐ pencil
- ☐ scratch paper
- ☐ freezer paper
- ☐ paper clips
- ☐ cutting mat or thick piece of cardboard
- ☐ utility knife (adult help suggested)
- ☐ scissors
- ☐ steam iron (adult help suggested)
- ☐ pillow cover
- ☐ cardboard
- ☐ fabric paint or acrylic paint mixed with textile medium
- ☐ flat, synthetic paintbrush
- ☐ pillow

 Steps

1 Write your word or name on scratch paper. Make it the size you want. The bigger it is, the easier it will be to cut out.

2 Draw an outline around your word to create a bubble. Make sure this new line is bold and if you have to, go back over your bubble drawing with black marker or darker pencil lines.

3 Cut out a piece of freezer paper a little bigger than your design.

4 Place the freezer paper, waxy-side down, over your word. Attach these together with paper clips so the paper doesn't wiggle.

5 Trace the bubble part of the word onto the freezer paper with a pencil.

Sharp tools! Have a grown-up help you with this step.

6 Place the freezer paper on a cutting mat or thick piece of cardboard.

7 Cut out the word with a utility knife and/or scissors to create a stencil.

8 Separate the scratch paper and freezer paper.

9 Remove the cover from the pillow and iron the stencil, waxy-side down, onto your pillow cover. Make sure that it's well ironed and there are no gaps along the edges where paint might seep under the stencil. This takes about a minute of ironing.

10 If you cut out any pieces from the middle of letters, such as the holes in the middle of the letters *o* or *a*, iron those down now.

11 Place a piece of cardboard inside the pillow cover. This will keep the paint from soaking through in the next step.

12 Paint inside the stencil with fabric paint or acrylic paint mixed with textile medium.

13 When the paint is dry, carefully remove the freezer-paper stencil and place the pillow cover over your pillow.

Family Tree

A *family tree* is pictorial keeper of memories. Drawing one and writing in lots of details will help you preserve family traditions and stories. Before getting started, you might want to interview a family member to learn the names of grandparents and even great-grandparents. While you may not include all the details on your family tree, you might also take notes on birth and marriage dates, towns your ancestors lived in, and even their jobs and hobbies!

You'll Need

- ☐ pencil
- ☐ watercolor paper (18" x 24") (45.5 x 61 cm)
- ☐ watercolor paint
- ☐ watercolor paintbrush
- ☐ cup of water
- ☐ towel
- ☐ fine point pen or marker

Steps

1 After collecting the names of family members, draw out your family tree on scratch paper. It may take a few passes to get it the way you want it.

2 Lightly sketch the family tree on your sheet of watercolor paper. Draw it large enough to leave room for adding names and details. Use a waterproof marker to go over the pencil lines.

3 If you have a family tree that's different from those shown here, that's fine! Simply change the tree to make it your very own. Each family is unique and special in its own way.

4 Paint in the tree with watercolor paint. Feel free to be creative in your color choices and the kinds of leaves, fruit, and flowers you might add.

4

Artful Cursive

Yarn Art

How about writing your name in 3-D cursive? Bring your name or favorite word (like peace, love, or friendship) to life with this colorful work of art made by bending and twisting pipe cleaners—like writing in air—and decorating the word with yarn. The finished words can be propped up against books on your bookcase, attached to a bulletin board, hung on a wall, or gifted to a friend.

Bend the Pipe Cleaners

1 Practice writing your word on a piece of paper. Make it large enough to trace with pipe cleaners.

2 Twist the pipe cleaners together to make a long string of them—long enough for writing your name or word. You can add more pipe cleaners as you go.

3 Bend the pipe cleaners to form the desired word.

Wrap with Yarn

1. Secure the end of the yarn to the beginning of the pipe cleaner by tying it into a knot.

2. Wrap the word with yarn. You can use multiple colors or one color. It's up to you! When you reach an intersection where the pipe cleaners cross, wrap the yarn around both wires to secure it in place.

3. When you reach the end of the word, secure the yarn with another knot and trim it.

4. Display your yarn art!

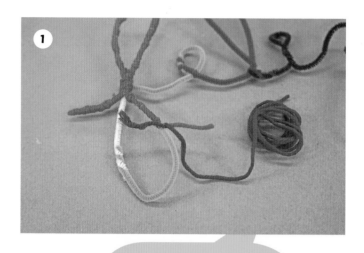

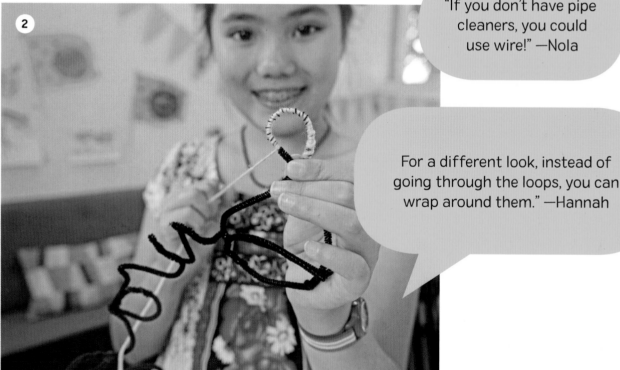

"If you don't have pipe cleaners, you could use wire!" —Nola

For a different look, instead of going through the loops, you can wrap around them." —Hannah

"If you don't want to see the pipe cleaner, you have to overlap the yarn a bit." —Nola

"When you're wrapping around a loop, you can thread the yarn through the loop a few times, loosely, and then tighten it." —Hannah

"If you don't mind having the pipe cleaner show through, choose a yarn color that complements the pipe cleaner color." —Ceclia

tip

To form looped letters, like a lowercase letter *e* for instance, twist the pipe cleaners together where they cross at the bottom of the letter. This will help the letter keep its shape.

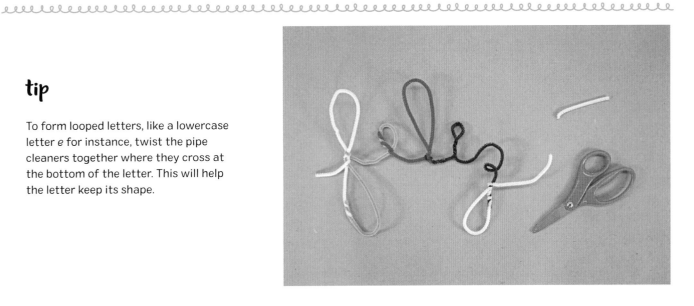

Repoussé Foil Art

Repoussé is a French word (pronounced reh-poo-*say*) that means "pushed up." The technique is often used in jewelry making, to give sheets of silver or gold a "pushed up" or raised design.

For this project, we'll make raised designs with aluminum foil and a glue gun. (I'll bet you never thought you'd be writing with a glue gun!) Use this technique to make a doorplate for your room, names tags to put on top of gifts, or any other ideas you dream up.

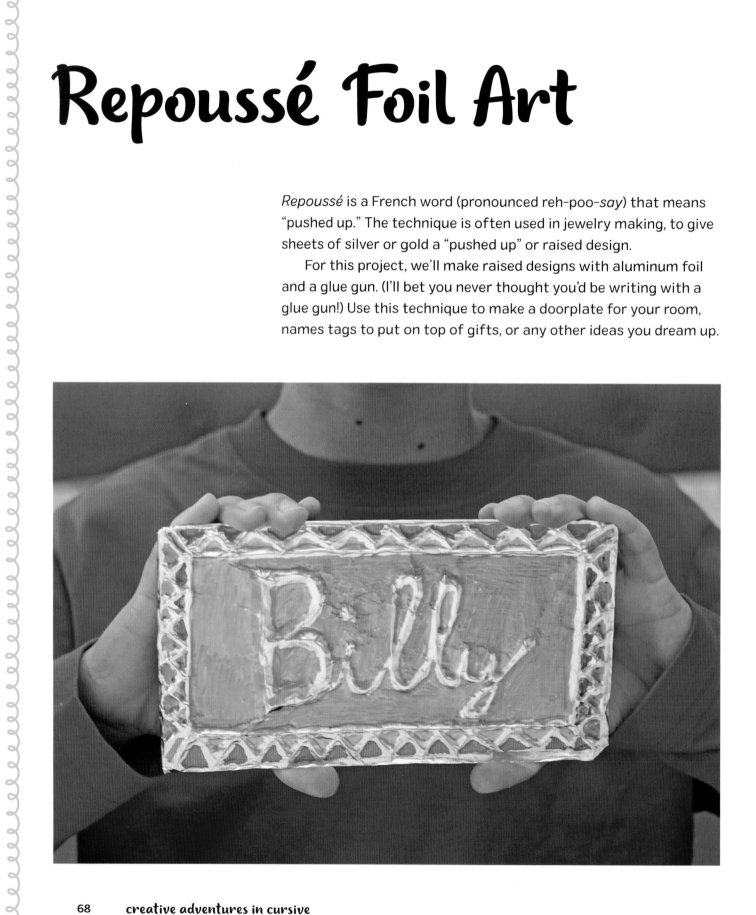

You'll Need

- [ ] pencil
- [ ] scratch paper
- [ ] cardboard, cut to preferred size
- [ ] low-heat glue gun and glue sticks
- [ ] heavy duty aluminum foil
- [ ] glue stick
- [ ] cotton swab
- [ ] permanent markers

Steps

1 Write your name or any words you like in cursive on a page of scratch paper with pencil until you have a design you're happy with.

2 Copy your cursive design onto the cardboard with pencil. Be sure that you make it big enough that you can easily go over the lines with the glue gun and still see the word. Add a decorative border in pencil, if you like.

3 Plug in the glue gun until the glue is hot.

4 Test your glue-gun writing skills: Trace over the words you wrote on the scratch paper to practice, before using it on the cardboard.

5 Are you ready? Trace over your word on the cardboard. Stop at the end of a letter if you need to take a break while writing.

6 To make your word pop, trace the border around it with more glue.

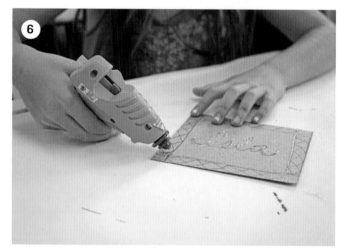

7 Allow the glue to harden. This should take less than a minute.

8 Cut a piece of foil larger than the cardboard by at least 1 inch (2.5 cm) all the way around.

9 Liberally cover the foil with the glue stick.

10 Place the foil on top of the design. Wrap the foil around the back of the cardboard and glue down the edges with the glue stick.

11 Starting in the middle of the design, gently rub the foil with the cotton swab, careful to not tear the foil.

12 Color in the design with permanent marker, leaving the raised areas shiny silver.

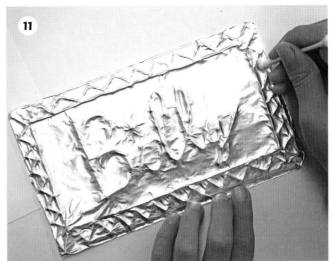

Word Pictures

Do you have museum-quality cursive? Now you can find out! This project is a fun way to turn your name, a friend's name, or any word you like into an abstract work of art. Use this technique to design the front of a birthday card or make a frame-worthy piece of art.

Steps

1 Write your name or another word on the paper in cursive.

2 Turn the paper and write your word again, crossing over the first name.

3 Continue turning your paper and writing your word, changing the size of your writing and even the style.

4 Keep going until your page is filled with words. Many of them will be unrecognizable. That's okay!

5 Fill in the closed spaces with marker. You could choose a special color palette such as all warm colors or all shades of blue or go rainbow and use a whole spectrum of colors.

artful cursive

VARIATION

Radiating Words

For another style of modern art, try this—it will show you the shape of your name in script!

1 Write your name in the center of a piece of paper.

2 Draw an outline around your name. Then, draw an outline around the outline.

3 Keep going, adding as many color outlines as you like. When choosing colors, you could decide on a color scheme such as shades of green or rainbow colors.

4 For a completely different look, color in only parts of your art!

These word pictures pop!

Ombré Lettering

Ombré is the French word for "shaded." It describes the blending of one color into another. In its wet state, watercolor is easy to blend and is pure magic to look at when it's dry. You can use this fun process just about anywhere that watercolor will stick!

You'll Need

- [ ] watercolor paper
- [ ] scissors
- [ ] optional: masking tape
- [ ] small, round watercolor paintbrush
- [ ] watercolor paint
- [ ] cup of water
- [ ] towel

 Steps

1 Cut the watercolor paper to the size you want. Tape it to your table to prevent it from slipping while you work.

2 Wet the paintbrush and swirl it into your first color. Write the first letter and the beginning of the second on the watercolor paper.

3 Before the paint has a chance to dry, rinse the paintbrush and load it with the next color.

4 Now, continue writing. Overlap the tail of the previous letter so that the colors blend. Make the rest of second letter and part of the third.

5 Continue in this fashion until all the letters are done.

6 Experiment with different kinds of paints to find one that you enjoy most. Some possibilities include liquid watercolors, tempera cakes, and watercolor cakes.

5

Celebrations

Cursive Cakes

tips

Use your favorite homemade or packaged cookies for this project. The directions for the icing appear below.

For a batch of cursive cookies, make the royal icing. Divide it into two bowls when it's ready: half for the background icing on the cookies and the other half for the writing. Cover the icing for the writing with aluminum foil or a damp kitchen cloth so that it doesn't dry out. Once you coat your cookies with the background color icing, give it 45 minutes to harden before writing on the cookies.

Mmmm. Cookies. What a delicious excuse for writing!

Add something special to the cookies you share with your friends by adding names, flourishes, or meaningful words written in icing! Choose short words and names that will fit on a cookie—big words require big cookies. (Did I hear you say "no problem"?)

Not only will your cursive cookies taste good, they'll look amazing, too.

Making Royal Icing

This recipe makes about 3 cups (700 ml) of icing, enough to ice and decorate about 24 cookies.

1   Stir the meringue powder and water together in a bowl.

2   Using an electric mixer, beat at low speed for about 7 minutes or until the icing forms stiff peaks.

3   Add 4 cups (1 L) of sifted confectioners' sugar* and continue to beat until the sugar blends in. Add more sugar for stiffer icing.

*No time for sifting? We rarely sift our sugar and the icing always turns out great.

You'll Need

- ☐ measuring cup
- ☐ mixing bowl
- ☐ ¼ cup (60 ml) of meringue powder
- ☐ ½ cup (120 ml) warm water
- ☐ electric mixer
- ☐ 4 cups (1 L) sifted confectioners' sugar*

You'll Need

- ☐ small bowls
- ☐ food coloring
- ☐ teaspoons
- ☐ small spatula
- ☐ piping bag(s) (More than one is helpful when you're working with different colors.)

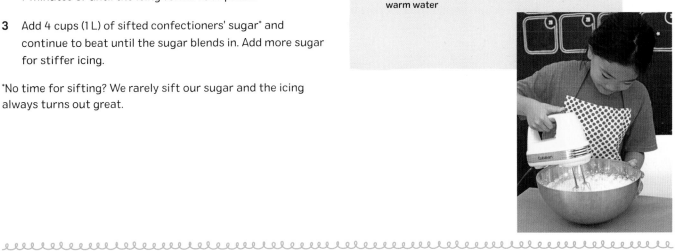

Icing and Decorating the Cookies

1   Decide how many colors you want, and divide your icing into separate bowls, one for each color.

2   Mix food coloring into each bowl of royal icing, a little at a time, stirring it in with a spoon or spatula to achieve the desired color.

For the Background

1. Using a spatula or the piping bag, cover each cookie with colored icing.

2. Allow the background to dry for 45 minutes.

For the Writing

1. Fill the piping bag(s) with royal icing. Twist the top(s) closed.

2. Practice: Write your word on paper with a pencil. Trace over the word with icing.

3. When you feel ready, write the word on your cookie.

4. Be creative—add dots, squiggles, or even math equations!

Decorating Tips

1. To minimize mistakes, write on your cookie with a toothpick first and then trace over that line with icing.

2. Here is the easy way to fill a piping bag: Place the empty piping bag in a cup, fold the edges over the cup's rim, and fill the bag with icing.

"It's fun because you can write anything you want. I did math equations because I love math!" —Exie

fun fact

This icing has the fancy name of royal icing. You might have seen it before as the decoration on a gingerbread house. It's a favorite for decoration because you can draw with it, you can color it, and it dries hard like candy. Royal icing got its name in 1840, when it was used to hold together an enormous 9-foot (2.74 m) wedding cake made for England's Queen Victoria and Prince Albert.

"You take a spoon and put it in the frosting, scoop it up, and jab it into the bag as far as you can until it's full, but not full to the very, very top." —Keo

"Put in 1 drop of blue and 2 drops of yellow to make green." —Keo

Notes on Piping Bags

Piping bags come with a variety of tips that allow you to make different kinds of decorations. The smaller the number on the tip, the finer the line you will be able to make. Small tips are best for writing. Follow the directions that come with your piping bag for assembly.

"You should twist the top of the piping bag so the frosting won't get out." —Keo

Birthday Balloons

Personalize your party by writing celebratory messages in markers or glitter on balloons.

Not your birthday? Then brighten a friend's day by mailing a birthday kit! Use your extra-fancy cursive style to make the balloons extra festive.

tip

To keep your balloon from wiggling while you write on it, place a loop of blue painter's tap on the back to temporarily to hold it to a table.

^{#1} Party Balloons

1 Practice writing your celebratory word or message on a piece of scratch paper.

2 Write your message on the balloon with permanent marker or paint pen.

3 Give the marker three minutes to dry.

4 Add a ribbon.

You'll Need

- [ ] scratch paper
- [ ] pencil
- [ ] helium-filled balloons
- [ ] permanent markers or paint pens
- [ ] ribbon

#2 Glitter Balloons

1. Practice writing your word or message on a piece of scratch paper.

2. Place your balloon on a table so it won't wiggle.

3. Write your word on the balloon with white glue.

4. Sprinkle the glue with glitter or candy sprinkles.

5. Place your balloons somewhere safe while the glue dries. Allow plenty of time to let it dry completely.

6. When the glue is dry, add a ribbon.

You'll Need

- ☐ scratch paper
- ☐ pencil
- ☐ painter's tape (paper tape)
- ☐ helium-filled balloons
- ☐ dry-erase markers
- ☐ white glue
- ☐ glitter or candy sprinkles
- ☐ ribbon

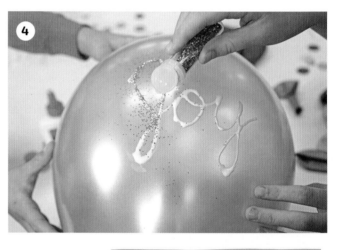

tips

Write the word large enough that you can easily re-create it in glue!

Glitter can be messy! It's a good idea to cover your work surface with newspaper before sprinkling!

#3 Mailing Balloons

1 Use a pump to blow up the balloon. Secure the end with a binder clip or chip clip.

2 Write your message on the balloon with the dry-erase marker after practicing on a piece of scratch paper.

3 Give the writing 3 minutes to dry.

4 Remove the binder clip and deflate the balloon.

5 Punch two holes in the card and thread a piece of yarn through the holes.

6 Tie the balloon in place with the yarn.

7 Write a birthday message on the card around the edges of the balloon.

8 Write the address on the envelope.

9 Place the balloon-card in the envelope and fill it with confetti before mailing.

You'll Need

- ☐ balloons
- ☐ binder clip or chip clip
- ☐ scratch paper
- ☐ pencil
- ☐ dry-erase markers
- ☐ blank card and envelope
- ☐ hole punch
- ☐ yarn
- ☐ scissors
- ☐ colored markers
- ☐ envelope
- ☐ confetti

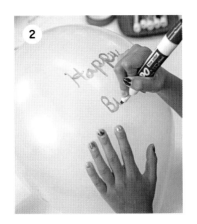

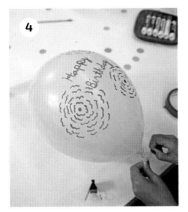

Message Chalkboard

Practicing your script with chalk is great—if you make a mistake, you can just erase it and start again. Chalkboards are so easy to make that you might want to make a few. They can be used for writing messages to family members, a dinner menu, or favorite quotes that keep you inspired. One thing I love to do is to turn old throw-away stuff into something new, and I like how this project can turn trash into treasure. Hunt for old framed art in thrift stores and yard sales; look for frames with smooth pictures and no glass.

"Although the texture will be different, if you don't have a roller brush, use a paintbrush." —Phévos

"Have fun!" —Grace

Paint the Chalkboard

1 Sand it: If your picture is bumpy, sand it first.

2 Paint a coat of chalkboard paint. Always paint in a well-ventilated space. Set up your painting station outdoors, or if you're inside be sure to open the door and windows.

3 Let the paint dry.

4 Paint on one more layer. Let the paint dry overnight.

Paint the Frame

1 If you want to paint the frame, use masking tape or painter's tape to protect the chalkboard surface.

2 Paint the frame with acrylic paint or spray paint.

Note: If you use spray paint, do this step outside or in a well-ventilated area. Spray several thin coats of paint to keep the paint from getting goopy or runny.

3 Allow the paint to dry completely before you pull off the tape.

4 Sand the edges if you want the original frame color to show through the newly painted frame.

"Wear an apron when you're painting so you don't get paint on your clothes." —Grace

Prepare the Chalkboard Surface

1 Before you write on the chalkboard, "season" it by rubbing chalk all over it. Hold the chalk sideways when you do this to cover a lot of surface at once.

2 Wipe the "seasoning" chalk away.

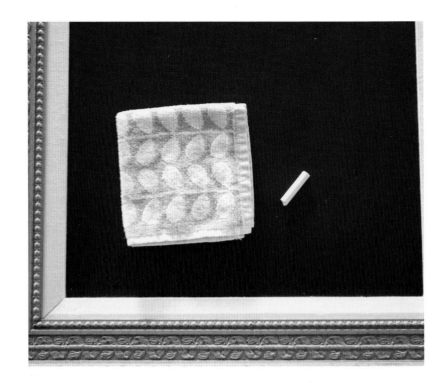

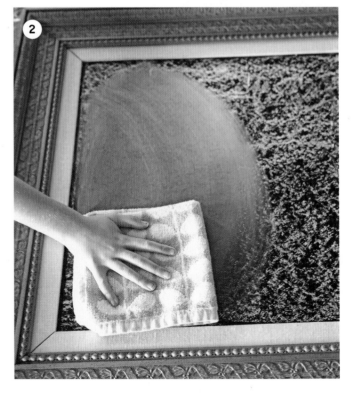

Decorate the Chalkboard

1 Write the word "Menu" at the top of the board in your best script.

2 Make a Monday through Sunday board by writing the days of the week down the left side of the board.

3 Make a daily menu board by writing all of the parts of the meal. For example, today's breakfast will consist of scrambled eggs, toast, mango smoothies, tea, and orange juice.

"If you press too hard, the chalk might break." —Phévos

Variation

Your chalkboard doesn't have to be framed. Paint an old canvas or wooden board with chalkboard paint and write anything that inspires you. Add vines and designs for an extra flourish (see page 16).

Gift Tag Collage

For this project, we'll use a brush pen. These are fun to use—like holding a pen, but they make marks like a paintbrush. Brush pens come in lots of colors and sizes, which make different widths of line. Try them out and see which ones you like best.

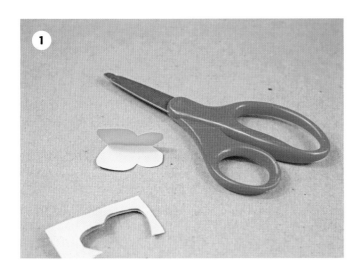

You'll Need

- [ ] construction paper in different colors
- [ ] pencil
- [ ] scissors
- [ ] brush pen
- [ ] white glue
- [ ] gift tags
- [ ] yarn

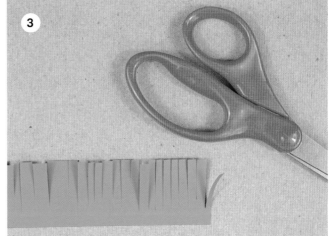

Steps

1 Fold a small piece of paper in half. Cut half a butterfly shape from along the fold line.

2 Open the butterfly and decorate it with the brush pen.

3 Cut blades of grass into a long rectangle of green paper.

4 Glue the grass and butterfly to the gift tag. To allow the butterfly to pop up, add glue only to its body.

5 Write your message with the brush pen.

6
Greeting Cards

Holiday Cards

The tradition of sending holiday greetings dates all the way back to the 1840s. It continues to be a wonderful way to connect with family and friends, both near and far. Why buy predesigned cards when you can make your own? Gather a stack of blank envelopes and cards of all shapes and sizes and invent your own seasonal greeting.

"One thing you need for this project is patience." —Harel

"Have a practice page to try writing on first because it's easy to make mistakes." —Harel

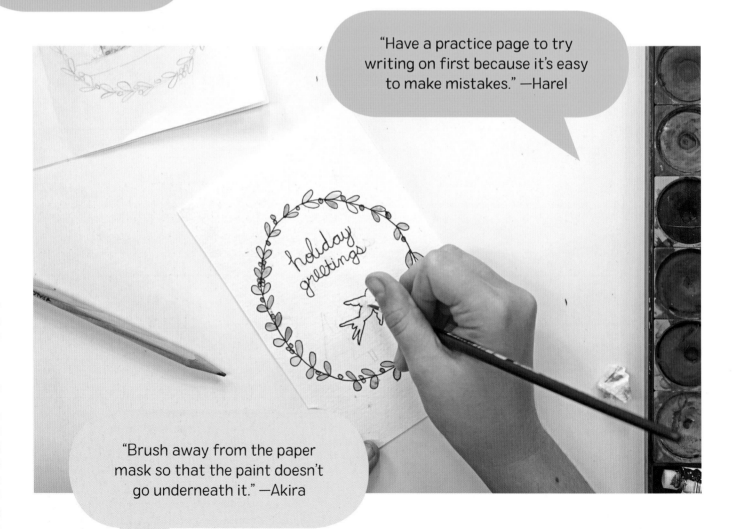

"Brush away from the paper mask so that the paint doesn't go underneath it." —Akira

You'll Need

- ☐ pencil
- ☐ scratch paper
- ☐ blank cards and envelopes
- ☐ fine-point black pen (such as a Micron pen)
- ☐ eraser
- ☐ watercolor paint
- ☐ round watercolor paintbrush
- ☐ cup of water

Steps

1   Practice writing your greeting on a piece of scratch paper. Then, write your greeting in your most elegant cursive on the front of your card with pencil.

2   Trace over the pencil with the fine-point black pen.

3   Erase any pencil marks.

4   Decorate the card.

Example Sheet of Messages to Write

HAPPY SPRING

WISHING YOU A VERY GREEN EARTH DAY

FOR A MAGICAL MIDSUMMER'S NIGHT

HAPPY NEW YEAR

HAPPY HALLOWEEN

PEACE ON EARTH

A SILLY APRIL FOOL'S

A SWEET VALENTINE'S DAY

HELLO WINTER

Pop-up Cards

These little cards have a big impact! While they may look complex, the secret is that they're easy to make with just a few supplies.

"This isn't a 5-minute birthday card. Give yourself time to finish this project." —Nola

tip

The cut lines need to be less than half the width of the card or they'll stick out when the card closes.

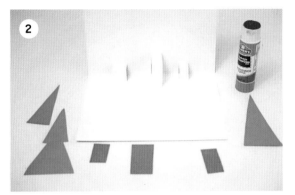

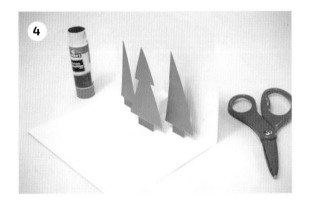

Basic Pop-up

1 On the folded edge of one of the cards, cut pairs of parallel lines. Each pair will become a pop-up element.

2 Open the card and push the cut piece into the card to create the pop-up.

3 Draw pictures on the card stock that you want to pop up.

4 Glue these images into place.

5 Add decorations to the foreground or background of the card.

6 Glue the cover card to the outside of the pop-up card.

7 Add your message with your best cursive.

Pop-up Cake Card

1. On the folded edge of one card, draw four lines with your pencil, increasing the length of each one.

2. Cut along the pencil lines. Crease the top of each of the three "rectangles." Flatten the rectangles out.

3. Fold the paper as shown in the photo. Open the card like a book. Reach one hand behind the card and push the three rectangular shapes toward the front.

4. Crease the paper so the cake holds its shape and forms a cake! Close the paper in half and give everything one more firm press.

5. Glue the cover card to the outside of the pop-up card.

6. Add embellishments and write messages in your very best script.

7. Cover the cake with fancy paper and add candles or bunting.

> Lightly write the cursive first in pencil before you use the pen, and if the pencil lines show after you trace it in pen, you can erase it." —Molly

"If you're a perfectionist like me, use a pencil to mark the colorful paper to match the shape of the pop out areas." —Becca

"Everything doesn't have to be 3-D. You can glue things to the background." —Ethan

Message Ideas

HAPPY BIRTHDAY!

HAPPY ANNIVERSARY!

HAPPY NEW YEAR!

HAPPY MOTHER'S DAY!

HAPPY FATHER'S DAY!

Photo Invitations

Possible Greetings

YOU'RE INVITED!

PLEASE JOIN US!

COME TO MY PARTY!

IT'S A BIRTHDAY!

JOIN US FOR A PARTY!

Party Details

DATE:

TIME:

LOCATION:

RSVP BY:

If you're planning a party, you'll need invitations. Of course, it's easy enough to make invitations online, but making your own invitation is so much more fun and gives you a chance to share your creativity. You can also use this technique to make birthday cards—just use an image of the birthday boy or girl and add words around the image to tell them something special or wish them well.

Steps

1 Take pictures of the people who should appear on your card. Use a plain white background, if possible.

2 Print a copy of the photo to fit the front of your cards.

3 Practice the message you want to write in script. Make sure it will fit in the place where you want to use it.

4 Use pens to write your message on top of the photo.

5 Cut out colorful patterned paper to embellish the image.

6 Add bright colors with paint markers or permanent markers.

Dot-Printed Thank You Cards

Sending a simple note to say thank you after receiving a gift or act of kindness can be as enjoyable for you as it is for the gift-giver to receive it. Good manners rock! Not only that, friends and family will love opening a personalized message from you.

You'll Need

- ☐ scratch paper
- ☐ black card and envelope pack
- ☐ Gold metallic, silver metallic, or white permanent marker
- ☐ gold or silver metallic acrylic paint
- ☐ pencil
- ☐ pencil with a new eraser
- ☐ paper plate
- ☐ scissors
- ☐ painter's tape

Steps

1 Practice writing your message in cursive.

2 Use the metallic permanent marker to write your message on the card.

3 To make a clean shape around your message, cut out a shape template and attach it to the card with a piece of painter's tape.

4 Squeeze about 1 teaspoon (5 ml) of paint onto the paper plate.

5 Dip the pencil eraser into the paint and make a dot pattern on the card and envelope. Make your dot pattern around and even overlapping the template. Wash the eraser in water to remove paint before it dries.

6 Remove the template when the paint is dry and write your message inside.

Message Ideas

THANK YOU!

A BIG THANK YOU!

THANKS!

THANK YOU VERY MUCH!

THANK YOU FOR EVERYTHING!

THANKS FOR YOUR KINDNESS!

"Use a new pencil because the eraser is flat and makes a perfect circle." —Audrey

"Make whatever shape you want." —Amelia

"Tape your stencil down to cover the word." —Amalia

What to Say in a Thank You Note

Begin with the greeting.

Dear _____ ,

Add the opening.

Thank you so much for . . .

I'm so grateful for . . .

Your gift of
_____ was so
generous. I love it!

Include a personal touch.

Thank you for being a great friend.

The gift is perfect! You know me
so well.

It was so fun to spend time with you
at the party.

I can't wait to see you again.

End with the closing.

Warmly,

Much love,

With gratitude,

All my love,

Your friend,

Cursive Review: Are you new to cursive writing, or maybe you need a refresher on how to write some of the letters? Use this template as is or make a copy to use alongside the projects in this book.

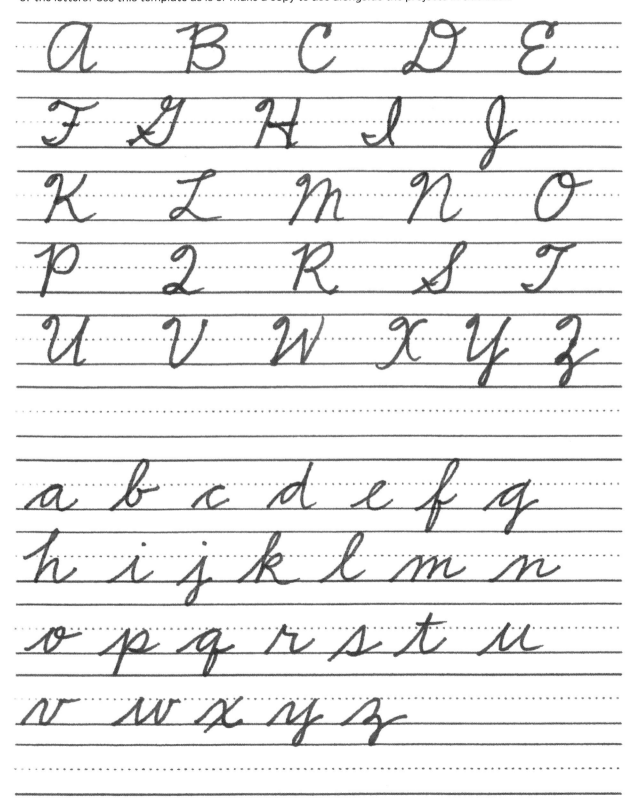

Acknowledgments

This book would not be possible without the guidance of my third-grade teacher, Mrs. Faye Ireland, who empowered my appetite for cursive writing.

Thank you to my editor, Judith Cressy, for conceptualizing this book and bringing it to life. I'm grateful for your flexibility, purposefulness, and passion for creativity. Big thanks to Erica Silverman, agent extraordinaire, everyone at Quarry Books who saw the beauty in this idea, David Martinell and your talented design team, and to the modern calligraphy inspiration of Maybelle Imasa-Stukuls. Endless gratitude to my family, friends, blog readers, and creative confidents: I'm indebted to you for the support, wisdom, and encouragement you've given me over the years.

Special thanks to friends, Aude Ismael and Cari Templeton, for sharing their bullet journals with me, and to the enthusiastic children whose faces and work grace the pages of this book: Adam Fong, Akira Hunter, Allie Jackson, Amalia Tormala, Amelia Yuan, Anna Kochenderfer, Audrey Davidson, Becca Rosenberg, Billy Lloyd, Cecilia Otani, Céleste Nicole, Connor Harrington, Daron Fong, Elise Chen, Emma Kochenderfer, Ethan Hong, Exie Stanat, Grace Chavez, Hannah Barnett, Harel Klinger, Isla Doorley, Katie Dorogusker, Keo Stanat, Lily Kochenderfer, Lucy, Naia Tormala, Max Nicole, Molly Rosenberg, Naomi Torres-Itoi, Nola Doorley, Parker Harrington, Phévos Raptopoulos, Rainey Ardoin-Hawkins, Senna Hong, Shakti Ann Kanyal, Zoe Mukamal.

Most of all I want to thank my cursive-writing kiddos, Nola and Isla, and my husband, Scott Doorley.

About the Author

RACHELLE DOORLEY is an arts educator, community builder, and founder of the popular creativity blog Tinkerlab. She is also the author of *TinkerLab: A Hands-on Guide for Little Inventors*, published by Roost in 2014. Rachelle studied costume design at the University of California, Los Angeles, and worked on Hollywood films before finding her true calling as an arts educator. After teaching elementary and middle school art, she earned a master's in arts education from Harvard, and then oversaw museum-based and education programs in Massachussets and California. Rachelle lives with her family in the beautiful San Francisco Bay area, where she teaches art, visual thinking, and creativity. She enjoys her sketchbooks, taking her kids on adventures, good friends, kawaii drawings, breakfast, hand-drawn letters, hikes in the woods, and ocean air.

Also Available:

Art Lab for Kids
978-1-59253-765-5

Art Lab for Little Kids
978-1-59253-836-2

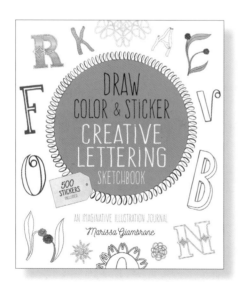

Draw, Color, and Sticker Creative
Lettering Sketchbook
978-1-63159-337-6

Hand Lettering A to Z
978-1-63159-282-9